D1599073

Speak This Not That

POSITIVE AFFIRMATIONS TO HAVE A BETTER DAY

Lynn Lok-Payne

WellMinded Media

Library of Congress Control Number: 2022905124

ISBN: 9781736459706 (ebook), 9781736459713 (paperback), 9781736459720 (hardcover)

Published by WellMinded Media
3941 Park Drive, Ste 20-559
El Dorado Hills, CA 95762
www.LynnLokPayne.com

Book Layout ©2015 BookDesignTemplates.com
Design by McKenna Payne

Printed in The United States of America
First Edition: 2022

To my daughter McKenna,
Thank you for editing, designing,
and being the sounding board for this book.
Your wonderful insight and inspiration
are invaluable. Life is better because of you!

Contents

Preface

THE GREATEST INFLUENCE ON our daily lives is our internal dialogue. It shapes everything from how we interact with others to the way we treat ourselves. Often, we aren't mindful of these mental conversations—many of which are noisy and disruptive. We dwell, ruminate, and worry about scenarios that never come to pass.

So here's the challenge. The mind is hard-wired to focus on the negative. In earlier times, this helped us to recognize and avoid dangerous threats, such as being chased by an animal. Today, we are still biased toward negativity. Many of these "thought threats" are just false narratives running wild. Even if there is some truth to these statements, we tend to make these stories seem far worse than they actually are. But with some attention, we can move from the worst-case scenario to a better place.

This book is designed to bring awareness to our self-talk and improve our thinking. It's a reminder to treat ourselves with compassion and encouragement. So how do we do this? First, by consciously considering what we are telling ourselves. How can change occur if we don't pay attention to the chatter in our heads?

Second is to revise and change our internal language to something more empowering. When we say phrases such as, "I'm not good enough," or "This won't work," we shrink our power, our worth. These limiting beliefs move us into victim mode, which makes us feel like we are not in control and narrows the possibilities we see in our lives. We wouldn't tell a friend they were not good enough, so why do we belittle ourselves? By making a simple change from "I can't" to "How can I?", we open the door to new opportunities.

Studies have shown that the brain can't tell the difference between real and imagined thoughts. By shifting our thinking, we can create new neural pathways to focus on the positive, change the way we perceive our experiences, and impact our reality.

Third, we can redirect our attention from scarcity to abundance. The best strategy I have found for this is to concentrate on gratitude and savor the good.

Finally, notice when speaking the words "I am." These two words are very important affirmations. When we state "I am...," this is the reality we create.

The words we use are extremely powerful. The stories we tell ourselves matter. When we shift our focus and intentionally choose the narrative we want for our lives, then we can thrive!

"Stop beating yourself up.
You are a work in progress,
which means you get there
a little at a time, not all at once."

— UNKNOWN

PART 1

Success

*"Whether you think you can
or you think you can't, you're right."*

— HENRY FORD

I can't do it.

INSTEAD, SPEAK THIS...

I can do this.

I just haven't done it yet.

By breaking down my tasks and goals
into small steps, I am able to accomplish them.

"If you can't fly then run, if you can't run then walk, if you can't walk then crawl, but whatever you do, you have to keep moving forward."

— MARTIN LUTHER KING, JR.

"It always seems impossible until it's done."

— NELSON MANDELA

It's not possible.

INSTEAD, SPEAK THIS...

I have faith in me.

It may take time, but I can achieve it.

Anything is possible.

My dreams are unrealistic.

INSTEAD, SPEAK THIS...

I believe in my dreams.

I will not let fear stand in the way of pursuing my dreams.

If I can imagine it, I have the ability to succeed.

"Too many of us are not living our dreams because we are living our fears."

— LES BROWN

"Your hardest times often lead
to the greatest moments of your life.
Keep going. Tough situations build
strong people in the end."

— ROY T. BENNETT

It's too hard.

INSTEAD, SPEAK THIS...

I can break it down into small steps.

With every action, I am moving toward my goal.

I have overcome struggles before
and I can do it again.

It's difficult to achieve success.

INSTEAD, SPEAK THIS...

In order to succeed, first I need to believe.

Success is attainable.

I am successful.

"Success means doing
the best we can with what we have.
Success is the doing, not the getting;
in the trying, not the triumph.
Success is a personal standard,
reaching for the highest that is in us,
becoming all that we can be."

— ZIG ZIGLAR

"Believe you can and you're halfway there."

— THEODORE ROOSEVELT

It's taking too long to achieve my goals.

INSTEAD, SPEAK THIS...

Every day I am getting closer
to making my vision a reality.

My goals are in the process of manifesting.

My faith is the greatest ally I have
in achieving my goals.

I don't know how to...

INSTEAD, SPEAK THIS...

I don't need to reinvent the wheel.
I can learn from what others have already done.

The answer is already out there,
I just have to find it.

How can I?

"Formal education will make you a living.
Self-education will make you a fortune."

— JIM ROHN

"All speaking is public speaking,
whether it's to one person or a thousand."

— ROGER LOVE

I'm bad at public speaking.

INSTEAD, SPEAK THIS...

I will learn from other speakers by watching their talks and reading books on speaking.

I am excited to share my ideas with others.

I know my subject and I speak with ease.

I don't have a purpose.

INSTEAD, SPEAK THIS...

When I pursue my interests, I find my purpose.

The world works in my favor when I live my purpose.

Every single person has several purposes.
Following our happiness is one of them.

"Having a purpose is the difference between making a living and making a life."

— TOM THISS

*"Everything you want is out there waiting for you to ask.
Everything you want also wants you."*

— JULES RENARD

I don't receive what I want.

INSTEAD, SPEAK THIS...

I am grateful for what I do have.

I have the power to reap my desires.

I can visualize what it would feel like to get what I want.

I'm never going to reach my destination.

INSTEAD, SPEAK THIS...

I can see and feel where I want to be.

Each step brings me closer to my dreams.

Happiness is the road trip, not the destination.

"Many of life's failures are people who did not realize how close they were to success when they gave up."

— THOMAS A. EDISON

"Work harder on yourself than you do on your job.
If you work hard on your job, you can make a living.
If you work hard on yourself, you can make a fortune.
Income seldom exceeds personal development."

— JIM ROHN

I can't get that promotion.

INSTEAD, SPEAK THIS...

I am confident in my abilities.

I will learn new job skills to advance my career.

I have unique strengths, such as problem solving or communicating well.

SPEAK THIS:

I can do it!

Believe in possibilities, dreams, goals.
Believe in your value, your purpose, your worth.
And don't worry about how it will be accomplished.
The "how" will come once you begin.

"The great secret of getting what you want from life is to know what you want and believe you can have it."

— NORMAN VINCENT PEALE

PART 2

Challenges

"Life is 10% what happens to us and 90% how we react to it."

— DENNIS P. KIMBRO

Challenges are bad.

INSTEAD, SPEAK THIS...

Challenges have taught me that I have the strength to overcome hard times and this resilience helps me in other areas of my life.

I have grown more from my challenges than my successes.

Challenges have made me a better person.

"When you come out of the storm,
you won't be the same person who walked in.
That's what this storm's all about."

— HARUKI MURAKAMI

"Reflect upon your present blessings,
of which every man has plenty;
not on your past misfortunes,
of which all men have some."

— CHARLES DICKENS

My life is terrible.

INSTEAD, SPEAK THIS...

Maybe my life is not as bad as I think.

Even with all my troubles,
I am still better off than most.

Hard times will pass.

I can't control my circumstances.

INSTEAD, SPEAK THIS...

I can control my reaction
and attitude toward the situation.

I focus only on what I can control.

I choose to take responsibility for my life.

"I am not a product of my circumstances.
I am a product of my decisions."

— STEPHEN COVEY

"Success is to be measured not so much
by the position that one has reached in life
as by the obstacles which he has overcome."

— BOOKER T. WASHINGTON

Life is hard.

INSTEAD, SPEAK THIS...

I can rise above my obstacles.

There are important lessons in hardships.
But there are also opportunities.

Good moments can still be found in hard times.

Nothing ever goes right for me.

INSTEAD, SPEAK THIS...

Life is benefiting me, even if I can't see it yet.

I shift my focus to what is working for me.

Tough times may be a sign to change my direction.

---

*"You're going to go through tough times — that's life.
But I say, 'Nothing happens to you, it happens for you.'
See the positive in negative events."*

— JOEL OSTEEN

"Problems are not stop signs,
they are guidelines."

— ROBERT H. SCHULLER

My life is filled with problems.

INSTEAD, SPEAK THIS...

Problems are a natural part of life that lead me to better solutions.

The world is working for me behind the scenes.

Challenges are lessons in disguise. What is it I need to learn?

I'm having a bad day.

INSTEAD, SPEAK THIS...

How can I improve it?

What has worked today?

What am I grateful for?

*"You can focus on things that are barriers
or you can focus on scaling the wall
or redefining the problem."*

— TIM COOK

"The greatest weapon against stress
is our ability to choose one thought over another."

— WILLIAM JAMES

I'm stressed.

INSTEAD, SPEAK THIS...

I don't have to do it alone.
I can ask for help.

When I concentrate on one task
at a time, I accomplish more.

My stress can be lowered through
deep breathing or taking a walk.

I'm stuck in negative thoughts.

INSTEAD, SPEAK THIS...

If a positive thought doesn't come easily,
I can reach for a more neutral thought.

Thoughts don't have to be static.
I can watch my thoughts transform.

I will revise my thinking
by making small changes.

"Positive thinking and negative thinking cannot operate at the same level in your mind, one needs to be the master and the one you feed it more will rule over the other."

— OSCAR BIMPONG

"Most of the important things in the world
have been accomplished by people who have kept on trying
when there seemed to be no hope at all."

— DALE CARNEGIE

There is no hope.

INSTEAD, SPEAK THIS...

I am courageous enough to see a different future.

There is a light at the end of the tunnel.

Tomorrow is a fresh start.

I give up.

INSTEAD, SPEAK THIS...

I can change my approach.

I have faith in a favorable outcome.

If I'm still dreaming of it, I can still achieve it.
And if my dream changes, it is okay to let it go.

"Never give up on something that you can't go a day without thinking about."

— WINSTON CHURCHILL

SPEAK THIS:

I am capable of handling any challenge.

Overcoming challenges is not easy,
but it can be done. Start here. Move forward.

"Life is about accepting the challenges
along the way, choosing to keep moving forward,
and savoring the journey."

— ROY T. BENNETT

PART 3

Change

"Everyone thinks of changing the world, but no one thinks of changing himself."

— LEO TOLSTOY

I can’t change.

INSTEAD, SPEAK THIS...

I am given the opportunity to adjust my mindset with each new day.

I can adapt. It’s innate in human nature.

I have within me the power to change.

"If you don't like something, change it.
If you can't change it, change your attitude."

— MAYA ANGELOU

"If you accept a limiting belief,
then it will become a truth for you."

— LOUISE HAY

I can't change my beliefs.

INSTEAD, SPEAK THIS...

I have the ability to shift my thoughts,
which help to create my beliefs.

My beliefs are meant to evolve.

As life changes, my ideas about the world realign.

I can't change my past.

INSTEAD, SPEAK THIS...

I can't alter the past, but I can create
a new vision for my life.

My past does not predict my future.

I accept my past because it holds the lessons
I need to build a brighter future.

"The secret of change is to focus all of your energy not on fighting the old, but on building the new."

— SOCRATES

"Don't spend a lot of time
imagining the worst-case scenario.
It rarely goes down as you imagine it will,
and if by some fluke it does,
you will have lived it twice."

— MICHAEL J. FOX

I fear change.

INSTEAD, SPEAK THIS...

I am safe in who I am and who I want to become.

I will envision and embrace positive outcomes.

The future no longer scares me because
I am equipped to handle any problem.

I can't forgive.

INSTEAD, SPEAK THIS...

Forgiveness is not for the other person.
It's for me to heal.

Forgiveness brings freedom.
It's never too late to forgive.

I will stop blaming myself
for past actions.

"Choose everyday to forgive yourself.
You are human, flawed, and most of all worthy of love."

— ALISON MALEE

SPEAK THIS:

Change starts within me.

Revise your thinking.
Believe that change is good
because it presents you with a world
of new opportunities.

"Yesterday I was clever, so I wanted to change the world.
Today I am wise, so I am changing myself."

— RUMI

PART 4

Doubt

"The only limit to our realization of tomorrow will be our doubts of today."

— FRANKLIN D. ROOSEVELT

I'm not good enough.

INSTEAD, SPEAK THIS...

I surrender the need to be perfect
and choose to stop comparing myself to others.

I love myself just as I am in this very moment.

I am enough!

"The most important day is the day
you decide you're good enough for you.
It's the day you set yourself free."

— BRITTANY JOSEPHINA

*"I've found that luck is quite predictable.
If you want more luck, take more chances.
Be more active. Show up more often."*

— BRIAN TRACY

Others are luckier than me.

INSTEAD, SPEAK THIS...

I create and repeat affirmations,
such as am lucky and I am successful.

I increase my luck by being optimistic
and expecting good outcomes.

Luck isn't something we get.
It's something we create.

I'm not smart.

INSTEAD, SPEAK THIS...

I am wise in my own way.

I remind myself of my strengths.

There are many different types of intelligence.

"You are braver than you believe,
stronger than you seem,
and smarter than you think."

— A.A. MILNE FROM WINNIE THE POOH

I am a mistake.
I made a mistake.

DO YOU HEAR THE DIFFERENCE?

I'm a mistake.

INSTEAD, SPEAK THIS...

My mistakes are what I have done, not who I am.

Every road to success is filled with missteps.

Mistakes are a guide to improve my future actions.

I'm a failure.

INSTEAD, SPEAK THIS...

Failure teaches us many things,
most of all resilience and compassion.

Failure doesn't define me. I may have failed
at something, but that does not make me a failure.

People often only remember the victories,
not the failures.

"The master has failed more times than the beginner has ever tried."

— STEPHEN MCCRANIE

"It is never too late to be
what you might have been."

— GEORGE ELIOT

I'm too old.

INSTEAD, SPEAK THIS...

Inspiration blossoms at every age.

Age is just a number. I will not give up.

Every day I am living is another day
to make my dreams a reality.

I'm too set in my ways.

INSTEAD, SPEAK THIS...

I have the ability to change my viewpoint.

I can switch up my routine.

I am open to embracing new experiences.

"When we become fixed in our perceptions,
we lose our ability to fly."

— YONGEY MINGYUR RINPOCHE

*"When everything seems to be against you,
remember that the airplane takes off
against the wind, not with it."*

— HENRY FORD

The worst always happens to me.

INSTEAD, SPEAK THIS...

I am working toward erasing doubt.

I will change worst-case scenarios
by visualizing best-case outcomes.

My thoughts of the future are not facts.
They are just what-ifs.

SPEAK THIS:

What's the best that can happen?

When doubt appears,
believe in something better.
Focus on the life you want to create.

"Doubts in your mind
are a much greater roadblock to success
than obstacles on the journey."

— ORRIN WOODWARD

PART 5

Perception

*"It's not what you look at that matters,
it's what you see."*

— HENRY DAVID THOREAU

They're wrong. I'm right.

INSTEAD, SPEAK THIS...

I expand my understanding
by listening to others' viewpoints.

There is always more than one perspective.

Will declaring I'm right truly make me happy
or should I let this go?

*"Though we see the same world,
we see it through different eyes."*

— VIRGINIA WOOLF

"Knowledge speaks, but wisdom listens."

— JIMI HENDRIX

I don't understand.

INSTEAD, SPEAK THIS...

I'm capable of learning
and open to new information.

When I truly listen, instead of thinking
about my response, I gain valuable insight.

When I look with fresh eyes,
I may discover things I previously missed.

Am I wrong?

INSTEAD, SPEAK THIS...

When I look at a matter from different angles, I gain clarity.

I release my ego's need to be right.

It's okay to change my beliefs and shift my perspective when necessary.

"You're going to find that many of the truths we cling to depend greatly on our own point of view."

— OBI-WAN KENOBI FROM STAR WARS, RETURN OF THE JEDI

"If you change the way you look at things,
the things you look at change."

— DR. WAYNE DYER

Why don't they see it my way?

INSTEAD, SPEAK THIS...

There is more than one way to view a situation.

Just because we see things differently doesn't mean either of us is wrong.

Agree to disagree.

These circumstances are holding me back.

INSTEAD, SPEAK THIS...

I can create a roadmap for the future I desire.

I am in charge of creating the path I want.

Nothing can hold me back.

"What you see and what you hear
depends a great deal on where you are standing."

— C.S. LEWIS

"Your problem isn't the problem,
it's your attitude about the problem."

— ANN BRASHARES

I'm not in charge of my own life.

INSTEAD, SPEAK THIS...

I am accountable for my life.

I can prioritize my activities to feel more in control.

In every step I take, I march toward the life I want.

SPEAK THIS:

I'm open to the possibilities in my life.

When we change our perception,
everything changes.

*"We don't see things as they are.
We see them as we are."*

— ANAÏS NIN

PART 6

Gratitude

"If the only prayer you ever say in your entire life is thank you, it would be enough."

— MEISTER ECKHART

I have nothing to be grateful for.

INSTEAD, SPEAK THIS...

I am grateful for my body, my breath, and my mind.

Gratitude multiplies. The more I embrace gratitude, the more gratitude will be revealed.

I place visual photos and mementos to remind me of people and things to be grateful for.

"When I started counting my blessings,
my whole life turned around."

— WILLIE NELSON

"Be thankful for what you have; you'll end up having more.
If you concentrate on what you don't have,
you will never, ever have enough."

— OPRAH WINFREY

I never have enough.

INSTEAD, SPEAK THIS...

I receive everything I need.

I appreciate what I already have.

I can imagine an abundant future.

I want many things that I don't have.

INSTEAD, SPEAK THIS...

I can focus on the good in my life instead of lack.

My life is filled with many small blessings.

Will having these things make me happier
in a year from now?

"It's a funny thing about life,
once you begin to take note
of the things you are grateful for,
you begin to lose sight
of the things that you lack."

— GERMANY KENT

"We make a living by what we get.
We make a life by what we give."

— WINSTON CHURCHILL

Why should I give to others?

INSTEAD, SPEAK THIS...

When I help my community,
I make a better place for everyone.

Giving expands my perspective and
makes me grateful for what I already have.

What I give multiplies. It's the butterfly effect.

SPEAK THIS:

I am blessed.

I intentionally seek gratitude
because gratitude leads me to joy.

"As we express our gratitude,
we must never forget that the highest appreciation
is not to utter words, but to live by them."

— JOHN F. KENNEDY

PART 7

Joy

"I believe that the very purpose of life is to be happy."

— THE 14TH DALAI LAMA

My life lacks joy.

INSTEAD, SPEAK THIS...

I shift my perspective to one of appreciation.

I'll make a list of what does make me happy.

Happiness is an internal choice I choose to seek.

"Let your joy be in your journey—
not in some distant goal."

— TIM COOK

"Optimists find joy in small things.
They enjoy sunsets, a good conversation
with a close friend; and they enjoy life in general.
They are more concerned with having many small joys
rather than having one huge joy."

— ROBERT M. SHERFIELD

How can I find joy?

INSTEAD, SPEAK THIS...

Once I am grateful for just one thing,
my heart opens to joy.

When I participate in activities
I like to do, joy follows.

Perform an act of kindness.

There is too much I need to do.

INSTEAD, SPEAK THIS...

I allow everything to flow with ease,
which puts me in my most productive state.

By simplifying and prioritizing my life,
I can lessen my stress.

I am learning patience.

"One of the best pieces of advice I ever got was from a horse master. He told me to go slow to go fast. I think that applies to everything in life. We live as though there aren't enough hours in the day but if we do each thing calmly and carefully we will get it done quicker and with much less stress."

— VIGGO MORTENSEN

"Life doesn't have to be perfect
to be filled with joy."

— ANONYMOUS

I always feel the need to put on a happy face.

INSTEAD, SPEAK THIS...

I don't have to be perfect.

It is healthy to experience all of my emotions.

It is essential to be my most authentic self.

Everybody on social media is happier than me.

INSTEAD, SPEAK THIS...

Most people only post their highlight reels,
so I really don't know what is going on in their lives.

If I knew other people's problems,
I would probably be happy to keep my own.

I shall not compare myself to others.

"Joy is not in things; it is in us."

— RICHARD WAGNER

"Miracles happen everyday,
change your perception of what a miracle is
and you'll see them all around you."

— JON BON JOVI

There is nothing good in the world.

INSTEAD, SPEAK THIS...

I am grateful that I am safe at this moment.

I choose to find the good.

When I change my way of thinking,
I see the wonders of life.

SPEAK THIS:

I choose joy!

Joy is a habit. Misery is a habit.
Which do you choose to walk with?

Happiness is not given to you.

IT IS CREATED BY YOU.

PART 8

Self-Love

“If your compassion does not include yourself, it is incomplete.”

— BUDDHA

I'm too slow.

INSTEAD, SPEAK THIS...

I work at my own pace.

I am carefully crafting my life.

It's better to do it right the first time than to fix mistakes.

"It does not matter how slowly you go
as long as you do not stop."

— CONFUCIUS

"I did then what I knew how to do.
Now that I know better, I do better."

— MAYA ANGELOU

I'm not doing it right.

INSTEAD, SPEAK THIS...

Each day I learn how to do it better.

Life is about failing, learning,
and getting back up again.

Fresh eyes bring in solutions.
Take a different approach.

I'm a bad person.

INSTEAD, SPEAK THIS...

I give myself compassion when I make mistakes.

I am capable of doing good things.

I can cultivate the person I want to become
by replacing unwanted behaviors with better choices.

"Good people can do bad things, make bad decisions.
It doesn't make them bad people."

— SONIA SOTOMAYOR

"Everything in the universe wants to be loved and accepted. Our personal work is to find the love and acceptance within ourselves."

— SHAKTI GAWAIN

I have trouble accepting myself.

INSTEAD, SPEAK THIS...

When I drop the woulda, coulda,
and shoulda, I find peace.

I accept all parts of me: the good, the bad,
and everything in between. All parts
serve a purpose, whether that is learning
love, empathy, or compassion.

I am whole as I am and worthy of goodness.

I don't like the way my body looks.

INSTEAD, SPEAK THIS...

I am grateful that my body
works hard for me every day.

Body comparison is a no-win situation
and doesn't add anything useful to my life.

I am dropping the negative obsessions
I have about my body and I realize
that self-love starts within.

"You have been criticizing yourself for years and it hasn't worked. Try approving of yourself and see what happens."

— LOUISE HAY

"Worthy now. Not if. Not when.
We are worthy of love and belonging now.
Right this minute. As is."

— BRENÉ BROWN

I'm not worthy of love.

INSTEAD, SPEAK THIS...

Open your heart and arms, then give yourself a hug.

I am worthy. I am valuable. I am lovable.

I am open myself up to receiving love
and release any blocks.

Others are better than me.

INSTEAD, SPEAK THIS...

I may be inspired by others' lives,
but that doesn't mean that my life is lacking.

I have my own unique qualities and strengths.

I am content with who I am and trust
who I'm becoming. I have the power
to cultivate who I want to be.

"Comparison is the death of joy."

— MARK TWAIN

"If you want to improve your self-worth, stop giving other people the calculator."

— TIM FARGO

I crave approval and validation from others.

INSTEAD, SPEAK THIS...

Other people's opinions of me
are none of my business.

I take back my power by trusting in myself.

I honor my needs because they move me
in the direction I wish to head.

I can't say no.

INSTEAD, SPEAK THIS...

No is a complete sentence. No excuse needed.

I respect myself enough to let go of any guilt that comes with choosing what's right for me.

I make myself a priority when I say no to something I do not want to do.

"People think focus means saying yes to the thing you've got to focus on. But that's not what it means at all. It means saying no to the hundred other good ideas that there are. You have to pick carefully. I'm actually as proud of the things we haven't done as the things I have done. Innovation is saying no to 1,000 things."

— STEVE JOBS

"Stop holding your truth; speak your truth."

— TIFFANY HADDISH

I don't speak up for myself.

INSTEAD, SPEAK THIS...

My feelings are significant, my voice is meant to be heard, and my ideas are worthy of being shared.

The more I speak my voice, the easier it becomes.

My well-being is more important than a few moments of discomfort when discussing my thoughts.

I'm a people pleaser.

INSTEAD, SPEAK THIS...

Putting myself first is not selfish.
It's important for my well-being.

I honor myself and set healthy boundaries.

I listen to my own inner voice
and stand up for myself.

"I can't give you a sure-fire formula for success,
but I can give you a formula for failure:
try to please everybody all the time."

— HERBERT BAYARD SWOPE

"The key is not to prioritize what's on your schedule,
but to schedule your priorities."

— STEPHEN R. COVEY

I have to...

INSTEAD, SPEAK THIS...

I have the freedom to make my own choices.

I drop any self-imposed language.

I want to.

I have no time for myself.

INSTEAD, SPEAK THIS...

I will make myself a priority and schedule me-time.

Taking care of myself is vital for my mental health.

I engage in activities that bring me joy,
including doing nothing.

*"Almost everything will work again
if you unplug it for a few minutes,
including you."*

— ANNE LAMOTT

SPEAK THIS:

I am enough!

I express self-love when I accept who I am.

"You are valuable because you exist.
Not because of what you do or what you have done,
but simply because you are."

— MAX LUCADO

Final Thoughts

THANK YOU FOR coming on this journey with me. I feel honored and blessed that you have chosen to read my book.

Here is what I have learned in my life. Everyone has their own interpretation of what **success** looks like. Just because someone else's idea appears different than ours, doesn't mean it's wrong.

Life is full of **challenges**, but these hardships make the good times more special by teaching us to appreciate our blessings. Accept what is. It is key to living a more peaceful life.

Change is always happening and when we learn to flow through transition instead of resist it, life is less of a struggle.

Everyone has **doubts**. The question is, "Will we let them control us?"

Everything in life is **perception**. When you change your focus, you gain more understanding.

Gratitude changes lives. When I started to appreciate each day, I discovered more of life's miracles.

Joy is what we all strive for. That doesn't mean we are happy all the time, but there are good things to be found in every moment.

Self-love is so important, not only for our well-being, but also for our relationships. We can't give to others what we do not give to ourselves. Embrace the wonder of you!

Love, Lynn

Speak This Not That

Every day we create our own personal reality with our thoughts and emotions. Use the next few pages to change your narrative and create better self-talk.

Index

About the Author

LYNN LOK-PAYNE is the award-winning author of *Wake Up! Change Up! Rise Up!, Practical Tools for Personal Transformation*, which won the prestigious Benjamin Franklin Silver Award. As a former CEO and founder of a multi-million dollar business turned author, Lynn motivates others to become the next chapter of who they are meant to be by creating a more empowering narrative for their life. When not writing, she can be found curled up with a good book, traveling to new locales, and attending concerts.

Sign up for weekly emails and free tools to help build your best life. If you enjoyed this book, I'd greatly appreciate a review.

CONNECT ONLINE

Social Media: @lynnlokpayne

Books and Website: www.lynnlokpayne.com